I0842720

Search for the Divine Prayer Yog Dhyan Mantra

Introduction: The search for the divine is a fundamental aspect of human existence. We have an innate desire to connect with something greater than ourselves, something that gives meaning and purpose to our lives. Throughout history, people have sought this connection through various means, including prayer, yog, dhyan, and mantra. These practices are not exclusive to any one religion or culture; they are universal, and they offer a path to spiritual growth and enlightenment.

Chapter 1: The Power of Prayer Prayer is a universal practice that is found in almost all religions and cultures. It is a way to communicate with the divine, to express gratitude, and to ask for guidance and blessings. This chapter explores the various types of prayer, including petitionary prayer, meditative prayer, and thanksgiving prayer. It also delves into the science behind prayer, including the power of positive thinking, the placebo effect, and the impact of prayer on our physical and mental health.

Chapter 2: The Practice of Yog Yog is an ancient practice that originated in India and has gained popularity around the world. It involves physical postures, breathing exercises, and meditation techniques that help to balance the body, mind, and spirit. This chapter explores the different types of yog, including Hatha Yog, Raja Yog, and Kundalini Yog, and the benefits of each. It also looks at the scientific evidence supporting the benefits of yog, including its impact on stress, anxiety, and depression.

Chapter 3: The Art of Dhyan Dhyan, or meditation, is a practice that is found in almost all spiritual traditions. It involves focusing the mind on a specific object, such as the breath or a mantra, to achieve a state of deep relaxation and inner peace. This chapter explores the different types of dhyan, including mindfulness meditation, lovingkindness meditation, and transcendental meditation. It also looks at the scientific evidence supporting the benefits of dhyan, including its impact on brain function, emotional regulation, and stress reduction.

Chapter 4: The Magic of Mantra Mantra is a powerful tool that is used in many spiritual practices to focus the mind and connect with the divine. It involves repeating a sacred word or phrase, such as "Om" or "Hallelujah," to create a vibration that resonates with the universe. This chapter explores the history and significance of mantra, as well as the scientific evidence supporting its use. It also includes a step-by-step guide on how to choose and use a mantra in your spiritual practice.

Chapter 5: The Journey Within The search for the divine is a journey that takes us deep within ourselves. It requires us to let go of our ego, our fears, and our attachments, and to connect with our true nature. This chapter explores the concept of self-realization, the process of awakening to our true identity, and the challenges and rewards of this journey. It also offers practical tips on how to deepen your spiritual practice and connect with the divine on a daily basis.

Chapter 6: Search for the Divine in Different Religions The search for the divine is a universal human experience that transcends cultural, geographical, and religious boundaries. While the specific practices and beliefs may vary between different religions, the ultimate goal is the same: to connect with a higher power and to live a more meaningful and fulfilling life.

Chapter 7: Secrets behind famous Saints in different religions Throughout history, there have been many famous saints and spiritual leaders who have inspired and guided people in their search for the divine. These individuals have left behind a legacy of teachings and practices that continue to influence and shape the lives of millions of people around the world.

Chapter 8: Famous sacred places in different religions in the world The world is filled with sacred places that hold deep spiritual significance for people of different religions. These places have drawn pilgrims and seekers for centuries, inspiring awe and reverence in all who visit them. Here are some of the most famous sacred places in different religions around the world.

Chapter 9: Similarities in different religions in the world Although the world's religions differ in their beliefs, practices, and rituals, there are many similarities that can be found across different faith traditions. Here are some of the key similarities that are shared by many religions around the world:

Chapter 10: Origin different religions in the world The origins of the world's religions are as diverse as the beliefs and practices they espouse. Some religions have ancient roots, while others are relatively new. Here are some of the origin stories of the world's major religions:

Chapter 11: Origin of Sanatan Dharma Sanatan Dharma, which is often referred to as Hinduism, is considered one of the oldest and most diverse religions in the world. Its origins are shrouded in mystery, and its history is marked by the intermingling of many different cultures and traditions. Here is a brief overview of the origin of Sanatan Dharma:

The Search for the Divine: Exploring Prayer, Yog, Dhyan, and Mantra

The search for the divine is a universal human pursuit that has been prevalent across cultures, religions, and civilizations throughout history. This search is driven by the innate desire of human beings to connect with something greater than themselves, to find meaning and purpose in their lives, and to seek spiritual growth and enlightenment.

Prayer, yog, dhyan, and mantra are some of the most powerful tools that have been used by people across the world to connect with the divine. These practices have been developed over centuries by various spiritual traditions and have proven to be effective in helping people to find inner peace, balance, and harmony.

Prayer is one of the most fundamental practices in almost all religions and cultures. It is a way of communicating with the divine, expressing gratitude, and seeking guidance and blessings. Prayer can be of various types, including petitionary prayer, meditative prayer, and thanksgiving prayer. The power of prayer lies in its ability to create a positive mindset and the power of collective prayer to bring about positive change in the world.

Yog is an ancient practice that originated in India and has gained worldwide popularity. Yog involves physical postures, breathing exercises, and meditation techniques that help to balance the body, mind, and spirit. It is a comprehensive system that offers a holistic approach to physical and mental health. The benefits of yog are manifold, including improved physical health, reduced stress and anxiety, and increased spiritual awareness.

Dhyan, also known as meditation, is a practice that has been used in almost all spiritual traditions to achieve inner peace and spiritual growth. Dhyan involves focusing the mind on a specific object, such as the breath or a mantra, to achieve a state of deep relaxation and inner peace. The benefits of dhyan include improved emotional regulation, increased focus and concentration, and reduced stress and anxiety.

Mantra is a sacred word or phrase that is repeated to create a vibration that resonates with the universe. Mantra has been used in many spiritual practices to focus the mind and connect with the divine. The magic of mantra lies in its ability to create a positive mindset and its power to transform consciousness.

The search for the divine is a journey that takes us deep within ourselves. It requires us to let go of our ego, our fears, and our attachments, and to connect with our true nature. The journey requires patience, persistence, and an open mind. It is about finding our own unique path to spiritual growth and enlightenment. The tools of prayer, yog, dhyan, and mantra are powerful allies in this journey, but ultimately, the search for the divine is a personal one.

In conclusion, the search for the divine is a universal human pursuit that has been prevalent across cultures, religions, and civilizations throughout history. The tools of prayer, yog, dhyan, and mantra have been developed over centuries and have proven to be effective in helping people to find inner peace, balance, and harmony. The search for the divine is a journey that requires patience, persistence, and an open mind. It is about finding our own unique path to spiritual growth and enlightenment.

Chapter 1: The Power of Prayer

Prayer is one of the most powerful tools for connecting with the divine. It is a practice that has been used for centuries in almost all religions and cultures. At its core, prayer is a way of communicating with the divine, expressing gratitude, seeking guidance and blessings, and cultivating a sense of peace and connection.

The power of prayer lies in its ability to create a positive mindset and to connect with something greater than ourselves. It is a way of acknowledging that there is a force beyond our understanding that is guiding and supporting us on our journey through life.

Prayer can take many forms, including petitionary prayer, meditative prayer, and thanksgiving prayer. Petitionary prayer is the most common form of prayer, where we ask for something from the divine. This could be anything from healing to financial abundance to guidance in making a decision. Meditative prayer is a more contemplative form of prayer where we focus on our breath or a particular thought to quiet our minds and connect with the divine. Thanksgiving prayer is a way of expressing gratitude for the blessings in our lives.

Studies have shown that prayer has many benefits, including reducing stress and anxiety, promoting physical healing, and increasing a sense of well-being. When we pray, our bodies release endorphins, which are natural painkillers and mood enhancers. This can help us to feel more relaxed and at peace.

In addition, prayer has the power to bring about positive change in the world. When we pray collectively, we create a vibration that can influence the world around us. This is why prayer circles and group prayer have been used throughout history to bring about positive change in communities and nations.

Overall, the power of prayer is undeniable. It is a way of connecting with the divine, cultivating a positive mindset, and creating positive change in the world. It is a tool that we can all use to find inner peace, guidance, and connection with something greater than ourselves.

Chapter 2: The Practice of Yog

Yog, also known as yoga, is an ancient practice that originated in India and has gained worldwide popularity. The word "yog" means union, and the practice of yog is about achieving a union of the body, mind, and spirit. Yog involves physical postures, breathing exercises, and meditation techniques that help to balance the body, mind, and spirit.

The physical postures of yog, known as asanas, are designed to stretch and strengthen the muscles, improve flexibility, and increase the flow of energy throughout the body. The practice of asanas also helps to improve posture and balance and can alleviate physical pain and discomfort.

Breathing exercises, or pranayama, are an essential part of yog. Pranayama involves conscious breathing techniques that help to regulate the breath and increase the flow of oxygen to the body. The practice of pranayama can help to reduce stress and anxiety, improve concentration, and promote relaxation and overall well-being.

Meditation is another important component of yog. The practice of meditation involves focusing the mind on a particular object or thought, such as the breath or a mantra, to achieve a state of deep relaxation and inner peace. The benefits of meditation include increased emotional regulation, improved focus and concentration, and reduced stress and anxiety.

The benefits of yog are manifold. It is a comprehensive system that offers a holistic approach to physical and mental health. The practice of yog can help to improve physical health, reduce stress and anxiety, and increase spiritual awareness. It can also help to promote inner peace, balance, and harmony.

Yog is a practice that is accessible to everyone, regardless of age, ability, or background. It is a non-competitive practice that encourages individuals to work at their own pace and listen to their bodies. The practice of yog can be done at home, in a studio, or even outdoors, and there are many resources available, including classes, books, and online videos.

In conclusion, the practice of yog is a powerful tool for achieving a union of the body, mind, and spirit. It involves physical postures, breathing exercises, and meditation techniques that help to balance the body, mind, and spirit. The benefits of yog are manifold, including improved physical health, reduced stress and anxiety, and increased spiritual awareness. Yog is a practice that is accessible to everyone and can be done in a variety of settings.

Chapter 3: The Art of Dhyan

Dhyan, also known as dhyana or meditation, is a practice that has been used for thousands of years to achieve a state of inner peace, clarity, and spiritual awareness. The word "dhyan" means contemplation or meditation and is a practice that is used to quiet the mind and focus on the present moment.

The practice of dhyan involves sitting in a comfortable position and focusing the mind on a particular object or thought. This could be the breath, a sound, or a mantra. The goal is to quiet the mind and become fully present in the moment, without judgment or distraction.

The benefits of dhyan are many. Regular practice can help to reduce stress and anxiety, improve concentration and focus, and increase overall well-being. Dhyan has also been shown to improve emotional regulation, increase self-awareness, and promote feelings of compassion and empathy.

One of the keys to a successful dhyan practice is consistency. Regular practice, even for just a few minutes a day, can have a significant impact on mental and emotional health. It is also important to approach the practice with an open mind and without expectations. The goal of dhyan is not to achieve a certain state of mind or enlightenment but rather to be fully present in the moment and to cultivate a sense of peace and inner stillness.

There are many different techniques and styles of meditation, and it is important to find a method that works for you. Some popular forms of dhyan include mindfulness meditation, mantra meditation, and visualization meditation. It is also helpful to find a quiet and comfortable space to practice and to minimize distractions.

In conclusion, the practice of dhyan is a powerful tool for achieving inner peace, clarity, and spiritual awareness. It involves focusing the mind on a particular object or thought and becoming fully present in the moment. The benefits of dhyan are many, including reduced stress and anxiety, improved concentration and focus, and increased overall well-being. Regular practice and consistency are key to a successful dhyan practice, and it is important to approach the practice with an open mind and without expectations.

Chapter 4: The Magic of Mantra

Mantra is a Sanskrit word that means "instrument of thought" and refers to a word or sound that is repeated during meditation or prayer. Mantras have been used for thousands of years in many different cultures and spiritual traditions as a way to focus the mind and connect with a higher power.

The repetition of a mantra is believed to have a powerful effect on the mind and body. When we repeat a mantra, we create a vibrational energy that can help to calm the mind, reduce stress and anxiety, and promote a sense of peace and well-being. The sound and vibration of the mantra also have a physical effect on the body, helping to reduce muscle tension and lower blood pressure.

In addition to its calming effects, mantras are also used to connect with a higher power or spiritual energy. The repetition of a mantra can help to cultivate a sense of reverence and devotion, and many people find that the practice of chanting a mantra helps to deepen their spiritual practice.

There are many different mantras used in various spiritual traditions, and it is important to find a mantra that resonates with you. Some popular mantras include "Om," "Om Shanti," and "Om Namah Shivaya." It is also important to approach the practice of mantra with an open mind and without expectations. The goal is not to achieve a certain state of mind or enlightenment but rather to cultivate a sense of peace, devotion, and connection.

Mantras can be chanted aloud or repeated silently in the mind, and the practice can be done at any time and in any place. Many people incorporate mantra into their daily meditation or prayer practice, but it can also be used as a way to calm the mind and promote relaxation during stressful situations.

In conclusion, the practice of mantra is a powerful tool for promoting a sense of peace, well-being, and spiritual connection. The repetition of a mantra can help to calm the mind and reduce stress and anxiety, while also promoting a sense of devotion and connection to a higher power. It is important to find a mantra that resonates with you and to approach the practice with an open mind and without expectations. Mantra can be incorporated into a daily meditation or prayer practice or used as a way to promote relaxation and well-being in stressful situations.

Chapter 5: The Journey Within

The search for the divine through prayer, yog, dhyan, and mantra is ultimately a journey within. While there are many practices and techniques that can be used to connect with a higher power, the ultimate goal is to develop a deeper understanding of ourselves and our relationship to the world around us.

This journey within involves developing self-awareness, exploring our beliefs and values, and cultivating a sense of inner peace and well-being. It requires a willingness to look within ourselves, to face our fears and insecurities, and to let go of limiting beliefs and negative thought patterns.

The journey within is not always easy. It can be a challenging and sometimes uncomfortable process, but it is ultimately a transformative one. Through the practice of prayer, yog, dhyan, and mantra, we can begin to develop a greater sense of self-awareness and a deeper connection to our inner selves.

One of the keys to this journey within is to approach it with an open mind and a willingness to learn and grow. We must be willing to let go of our preconceived notions and beliefs and be open to new perspectives and ideas. It is also important to have patience and compassion for ourselves as we navigate this journey.

The journey within is not a one-time event, but rather an ongoing process of self-discovery and growth. It requires a commitment to regular practice and a willingness to persevere through the challenges and setbacks.

In conclusion, the search for the divine is ultimately a journey within. It involves developing self-awareness, exploring our beliefs and values, and cultivating a sense of inner peace and well-being. This journey requires a willingness to look within ourselves, to face our fears and insecurities, and to let go of limiting beliefs and negative thought patterns. With patience, compassion, and a commitment to regular practice, we can begin to connect with our inner selves and develop a deeper understanding of our relationship to the world around us.

Chapter 6: Search for the Divine in Different Religions

The search for the divine is a universal human experience that transcends cultural, geographical, and religious boundaries. While the specific practices and beliefs may vary between different religions, the ultimate goal is the same: to connect with a higher power and to live a more meaningful and fulfilling life.

In Christianity, prayer is a fundamental practice that involves communicating with God and seeking guidance and support. Christians also believe in the power of worship and the importance of developing a personal relationship with Jesus Christ.

In Islam, the practice of prayer is central to the faith and involves performing ritual prayers five times a day. Muslims also believe in the importance of surrendering to the will of Allah and following the teachings of the Prophet Muhammad.

In Hinduism, the practice of yog and dhyan are important tools for connecting with the divine. Hindus believe in the existence of multiple deities and the importance of karma, or the concept that our actions have consequences that affect our future lives.

In Buddhism, the practice of meditation is a key component of the search for enlightenment. Buddhists seek to cultivate a sense of inner peace and compassion for all beings, and they believe in the importance of letting go of attachment and desire.

In Judaism, the practice of prayer involves connecting with God and seeking guidance and support. Jews also believe in the importance of following the commandments and living a moral and ethical life.

In Sikhism, the practice of chanting mantras and engaging in selfless service to others are important aspects of the search for the divine. Sikhs believe in the importance of living a life of service, compassion, and humility.

In conclusion, the search for the divine is a fundamental aspect of many different religions. While the specific practices and beliefs may vary, the ultimate goal is the same: to connect with a higher power and to live a more meaningful and fulfilling life. By exploring the practices and beliefs of different religions, we can gain a deeper understanding of the universal human experience of seeking spiritual connection and fulfillment.

Chapter 7: Secrets behind famous Saints in different religions

Throughout history, there have been many famous saints and spiritual leaders who have inspired and guided people in their search for the divine. These individuals have left behind a legacy of teachings and practices that continue to influence and shape the lives of millions of people around the world.

In Christianity, Saint Teresa of Avila is known for her teachings on prayer and contemplation. She believed that the search for the divine required a deep and personal relationship with God, and that prayer was the key to developing this relationship.

In Islam, the Prophet Muhammad is revered as the founder of the religion and the ultimate example of a faithful and compassionate servant of God. His teachings on the importance of prayer, charity, and self-discipline continue to guide Muslims today.

In Hinduism, the saint Ramakrishna is known for his devotion to the goddess Kali and his teachings on the importance of spiritual practice and selfless service to others. His disciple, Swami Vivekananda, brought his teachings to the West and inspired a generation of spiritual seekers.

In Buddhism, the Dalai Lama is a revered spiritual leader and the embodiment of compassion and wisdom. His teachings on mindfulness, meditation, and the importance of developing inner peace and compassion have inspired millions around the world.

In Judaism, Rabbi Nachman of Breslov is known for his teachings on joy and the importance of finding happiness in every moment. He believed that the search for the divine required a deep connection to the present moment and a willingness to let go of fear and anxiety.

In Sikhism, Guru Nanak is revered as the founder of the religion and a model of humility, compassion, and service. His teachings on the importance of living a life of service to others and cultivating a deep sense of devotion to the divine continue to guide Sikhs today.

In conclusion, the lives and teachings of famous saints in different religions offer insight into the universal human experience of seeking spiritual connection and fulfillment. These individuals have left behind a legacy of wisdom and guidance that continues to inspire and guide people around the world in their search for the divine. Through their teachings and examples, we can learn valuable lessons about the importance of spiritual practice, selfless service, and compassion for all beings.

Chapter 8: Famous sacred places in different religions in the world

The world is filled with sacred places that hold deep spiritual significance for people of different religions. These places have drawn pilgrims and seekers for centuries, inspiring awe and reverence in all who visit them. Here are some of the most famous sacred places in different religions around the world.

In Christianity, the Holy Land is a collection of sites in Israel and Palestine that are central to the religion. The most famous of these is the Church of the Holy Sepulchre in Jerusalem, which is believed to be the site where Jesus was crucified and resurrected.

In Islam, the Kaaba in Mecca, Saudi Arabia is the most sacred site in the religion. Muslims believe that it was built by the Prophet Ibrahim and is the place where Adam and Eve first prayed after their expulsion from the Garden of Eden. Millions of Muslims make the pilgrimage to Mecca every year for the Hajj, a requirement of the faith.

In Hinduism, the city of Varanasi in India is considered one of the most sacred places in the religion. It is believed to be the abode of Lord Shiva and the place where the river Ganges flows into the plains. It is also a place of pilgrimage and is believed to be the site of the ancient city of Kashi, the "City of Light."

In Buddhism, Bodh Gaya in India is the most sacred place in the religion. It is believed to be the site where the Buddha attained enlightenment, and the Mahabodhi Temple that stands there today is a UNESCO World Heritage Site.

In Judaism, the Western Wall in Jerusalem is one of the most sacred sites in the religion. It is believed to be the last remaining part of the Second Temple and is a place of prayer and pilgrimage for Jews around the world.

In Sikhism, the Golden Temple in Amritsar, India is the most sacred site in the religion. It is a place of worship and pilgrimage for Sikhs, and is known for its distinctive golden dome and surrounding pool of water.

In conclusion, the world is filled with sacred places that are central to the spiritual beliefs and practices of people of different religions. These places offer a connection to the divine and a sense of awe and reverence that can inspire and guide seekers in their search for the divine. Through visiting these sacred places and learning about their histories and traditions, we can gain a deeper understanding of the universal human experience of seeking spiritual connection and fulfillment.

Chapter 9: Similarities in different religions in the world

Although the world's religions differ in their beliefs, practices, and rituals, there are many similarities that can be found across different faith traditions. Here are some of the key similarities that are shared by many religions around the world:

1. Belief in a higher power: Almost all religions share the belief in a higher power, whether it is a single god or a collection of deities. This higher power is often considered to be the creator of the universe and the ultimate source of all things.
2. Ethical codes: Most religions have a set of ethical codes that govern how followers should behave in their daily lives. These codes often include rules about how to treat others, the importance of honesty, and the need to avoid harmful actions.
3. Practices and rituals: Many religions have specific practices and rituals that are used to connect with the divine. These can include prayer, meditation, and offerings to the divine.
4. The search for meaning and purpose: Most religions seek to answer the big questions about the meaning and purpose of life, and the nature of the universe. They offer teachings and insights into the human experience, and ways to find fulfillment and happiness.
5. A focus on community: Religion often provides a sense of community and belonging to its followers. Through shared practices, rituals, and beliefs, followers can find a sense of connection and support with others who share their beliefs.
6. The importance of compassion and love: Many religions place a strong emphasis on compassion

and love for all beings, and on the importance of treating others with kindness and respect.

In conclusion, while there are many differences among the world's religions, there are also many similarities. By focusing on these commonalities, we can find ways to connect with others from different faith traditions and build bridges of understanding and compassion. We can also learn valuable lessons about the human experience of seeking meaning and purpose, and how to live a fulfilling and meaningful life.

Chapter 10: Origin different religions in the world

The origins of the world's religions are as diverse as the beliefs and practices they espouse. Some religions have ancient roots, while others are relatively new. Here are some of the origin stories of the world's major religions:

1. Hinduism: Hinduism is considered one of the oldest religions in the world, with roots going back more than 5,000 years. Its origins are found in the Vedas, a collection of sacred texts that were written in ancient India. The religion evolved over time to include a wide variety of practices and beliefs, including the worship of many deities and the concepts of karma and reincarnation.
2. Buddhism: Buddhism was founded by Siddhartha Gautama, a prince in ancient India who renounced his wealth and status to seek enlightenment. After years of meditation and self-reflection, he became the Buddha, or "awakened one," and began teaching his followers about the nature of suffering and how to find liberation from it.
3. Judaism: Judaism is one of the oldest monotheistic religions, with its roots in ancient Israel. It was founded by Abraham, who is considered the father of the Jewish people, and its early teachings were recorded in the Torah, the first five books of the Hebrew Bible.
4. Christianity: Christianity was founded by Jesus of Nazareth, a Jewish preacher who lived in ancient Palestine. He taught a message of love and compassion, and his teachings were recorded in the New Testament of the Christian Bible.
5. Islam: Islam was founded by the Prophet Muhammad, who lived in Arabia in the 7th century. He received revelations from the angel

Gabriel, which were recorded in the Quran, the holy book of Islam. His teachings emphasized the importance of submission to God and the need to follow the Five Pillars of Islam.

6. Sikhism: Sikhism was founded by Guru Nanak, a spiritual teacher who lived in India in the 15th century. His teachings emphasized the importance of meditation, selfless service, and the belief in one God.

In conclusion, the origins of the world's religions are as diverse as the religions themselves. Each religion has its own unique story, teachings, and practices, but they all share a common goal of helping people find meaning and purpose in their lives, and a connection to something greater than themselves. Understanding the origins of different religions can help us appreciate the diversity of human culture and belief, and find common ground with people from different backgrounds and traditions.

Chapter 11: Origin of Sanatan Dharma

Sanatan Dharma, which is often referred to as Hinduism, is considered one of the oldest and most diverse religions in the world. Its origins are shrouded in mystery, and its history is marked by the intermingling of many different cultures and traditions. Here is a brief overview of the origin of Sanatan Dharma:

The term "Sanatan Dharma" is derived from the Sanskrit language, with "Sanatan" meaning eternal, and "Dharma" meaning duty, righteousness, or religion. It is based on a vast and complex body of texts known as the Vedas, which are believed to have been passed down orally from generation to generation for thousands of years before being written down.

The Vedas are a collection of sacred texts that contain a wide range of philosophical, religious, and spiritual teachings. They are considered the foundation of Sanatan Dharma, and are the oldest known Hindu scriptures. The Vedas are divided into four main sections: the Rigveda, the Yajurveda, the Samaveda, and the Atharvaveda.

The Rigveda, which is the oldest of the four Vedas, is believed to have been composed around 1500 BCE. It contains hymns and prayers that are dedicated to various deities, and is considered to be one of the oldest religious texts in the world.

Over time, the Vedas were supplemented by other texts, including the Upanishads, which contain philosophical and spiritual teachings, and the Puranas, which contain myths, legends, and stories about various deities.

Sanatan Dharma has evolved over time, and has been influenced by a wide range of cultures and traditions, including Buddhism, Jainism, and Islam. Despite this diversity, there are a few core beliefs and practices that are shared by most followers of Sanatan Dharma, including the belief in karma, reincarnation, and the existence of a single divine force that underlies all of creation.

In conclusion, the origin of Sanatan Dharma is a complex and multifaceted story, marked by the intermingling of many different cultures and traditions. Its core beliefs and practices have evolved over time, and continue to be shaped by the ongoing spiritual and philosophical exploration of its followers. Despite its vast and diverse history, Sanatan Dharma remains one of the world's most vibrant and dynamic religious traditions.

Conclusion:
The search for the divine is a never-ending journey that requires patience, persistence, and an open mind. Prayer, yog, dhyan, and mantra are powerful tools that can help us on this journey, but ultimately, the search for the divine is a personal one. It is about finding our own unique path to spiritual growth and enlightenment. This book is a guide to help you on your journey, but the true search for the divine begins within.

"Thank You"
Search for the Divine Prayer Yog Dhyan Mantra by Ajay Gautam
Book Copyright © 2023 Ajay Gautam